DUST BLOWN SIDE OF THE JOURNEY

THE HUGH MACLENNAN POETRY SERIES

Editors: Allan Hepburn and Carolyn Smart

TITLES IN THE SERIES

Dust Blown Side
of the Journey

Eleonore Schönmaier

McGill-Queen's University Press
Montreal & Kingston • London • Chicago

ISBN 978-0-7735-5013-1 (paper)
ISBN 978-0-7735-5014-8 (ePDF)
ISBN 978-0-7735-5015-5 (ePUB)

Legal deposit first quarter 2017
Bibliothèque nationale du Québec

Printed in Canada on acid-free paper that is 100% ancient forest
free (100% post-consumer recycled), processed chlorine free

McGill-Queen's University Press acknowledges the support of the
Canada Council for the Arts for our publishing program. We also
acknowledge the financial support of the Government of Canada
through the Canada Book Fund for our publishing activities.

Library and Archives Canada Cataloguing in Publication

Schönmaier, Eleonore, author
    Dust blown side of the journey / Eleonore Schönmaier.

    (The Hugh MacLennan poetry series)
    Poems.
    Issued in print and electronic formats.
    ISBN 978-0-7735-5013-1 (paper). –
    ISBN 978-0-7735-5014-8 (ePDF). –
    ISBN 978-0-7735-5015-5 (ePUB)

    I. Title. II. Series: Hugh MacLennan poetry series

    PS8587.C4585D88 2017   C811'.54   C2016-907737-3
                                                C2016-907738-1

This book was typeset by Marquis Interscript
in 9.5/13 New Baskerville.

For Bruce

CONTENTS

ἐὰν μὴ ἔλπηται ἀνέλπιστον, οὐκ ἐξευρήσει,
ἀνεξερεύνητον ἐὸν καὶ ἄπορον.

HERAKLEITOS

the tunnel
exit you'll be
there waiting for
me sitting on a wooden
crate at the side

of the tracks
you'll be holding
a bowl of
pumpkin soup
you cooked on a camp

stove by the dust
blown side of the
journey. my hands
and face will be
dirty and you'll

gently touch
my cheek.
you'll give
me your spoon.
if you're not

there waiting I'll find
the crate and I'll sit there
and wait for you, even
when the stars
have been wiped from

their slate, and the moon
is a stained
white plate cracked
and crowded
with insects. I'll

sit on the half broken
boards where the faded
words once said *oranges*
and there we'll meet. I'll give
you my hands

PARADISE EVACUATED

István used to survey

the land with red stakes
and the stars at night dipped
their faces into his sight line

we are all far, far away from
each other and also very
close: Paradise is real

you can visit any time
if only for a perfect day or
if only in your memory

years ago István and my sister
swam out to greet me
and my lover in our

canoe: my sister had an
orange in her swimsuit
and István had a cold

beer in his shorts: he
reminded me of this
yesterday on the phone

when we talked about
his bone cancer and
the local wildfires before

the lines burned down

the spaces are dreams
of architects brought
into being and are workable
and visual and no one is dripping
blood on the floor and no one is
screaming and a young
woman hasn't just
been hauled in by
police in a full
straitjacket only because
she wanted to sit alone
on a gravel road
in the northern bush
and the director
doesn't bring in
her pedigree dogs for
oxygen therapy
and a young man
isn't in hospital
with a broken leg
for a month because he's
homeless and it's the only
way he'll heal, and
a man isn't in
an isolation room for
weeks just waiting
to hear if
he has tuberculosis
(he doesn't) and a man

isn't white with fear
over the unknown
toilet and a woman
isn't afraid to
feed her toddler a grape
because she's never
seen this fruit
before and there's sorrow
and suffering here
but it's well-groomed as if
death is a party for
people in the
other room

THE MORNING AFTER

the ambulance ride
her kitchen floor
was covered in

her lover's chest hair
bits of yellow plastic,
gauze, electrodes and

on her piano keyboard
she found one
blue glove

RISK

The doorbell has been cut
and the only way to gain entrance is
to stand in the middle of

the bridge jumping up
and down, but this is futile
until you begin to sing

and from the upper-floor
window our friend looks
down and lets us in. We sit

at the window and touch
the seashells in their bowl
and our friend picks up

the conch, leans out
the window and lets it sound
so the canal boat captains

travelling below search
for the unseen and
in their confusion they

risk colliding with
the visible. Another
friend arrives and we

wine and dine and play
the Steinway as the storm
quavers against the roof

and the wind and jets flying
low overhead sound
alike as we journey closer

into our true selves
and you talk about
the wind quintet

you're composing
where the clarinet
will sound off stage

and you say all of us
are in your music
along with our missing

friend and walking home
I say, "I've had other
devoted friends before

but this evening's circle
are my soulmates"
and you say, "It's the

soulmates and not
the others who will
break our hearts."

LATE NIGHT ON VALENTINE'S DAY
IN THE SILENT COMPARTMENT

I'm reading *Risking
Everything*. The man next

to me in the fuzzy pig
outfit undoes his zipper

pulls out his phablet
and reads, "The people

in Leiden have the best
sex-life in the country."

He looks at me and
says, "Are you from

Leiden?" "Of course,"
I say. His girlfriend

says, "Boofie don't talk
to strangers." She's wearing

a green frizzy wig
matching gloves and

leggings and she turns
toward me and says, "With

your blue dress you
could have joined us."

I exit at one stop
past Leiden.

month of September is
when the sun
plunges into
the sea like a
trash can lid
seeking its own long
dark sleep
you meet your
lover in an attic
room and when you
stand up you smash
your skull
against the ceiling
and you do this twice
the light
floods through
the dormers
and the pain knocks
your thoughts off
of their tracks
you're too
deeply in love
and the church bells
ring not for mass
but for your own
over exuberance
the doctor says
it's only a small
cut in your scalp

and your brain
will be fine
you don't
dare ask
him about
your heart and how
it will beat
in the years
to come
the blood
soaked into your
hair and later
your lover finds
your soiled gauze
on the bedroom floor
and holds it to his lips

from September. a woman
walks over the bridge
pushing a full-in-blossom
cherry tree
horizontal on her bike:
where in the city will
she plant this? a patch of soil
large enough for
a life. I turn
toward the splashing
as a kayak whooshes
under the bridge: I want to
climb on board. river
lined with trees shedding
their chestnuts, fruit split
open on the curbside

MIRROR ORCHIDS

they line our cliff edged
trail, pollinated
by deception

and in the next
village we stand
at the blind

corner, next to
the no entry
sign, beneath the round

red-trimmed mirror
and we use this
for a self-portrait, catching

ourselves at these crossroads
with our eyebrows
raised in laughter

IN LOVE

they dined under
the Judas tree
storks high

in their nests
and the sperm
finding her egg

is not his while
he photographs
Europe's oldest

slave market
just down
the street

MISSING

the signs have
fallen and only
the frames
remain: they
contain within
their limits
the sea and sky
and an occasional
snail: missing is the
warning about
cliff edges

I'm lying on the rock
as if it's my own
bed. the stone
has more curve
than me, but
I'm lying flat
since this is only
a fraction
of the vast orbiting
earth. the granite
absorbs the sun rays
and I embrace
the warmth, while
my face is being pock-
marked by the grit
of the real
and at night
indoors a red
ant bites my right
breast and wakes
me up. last
night it was the inside
of my left knee
seasalt flavours
my skin, and the surf
shudders against
the shore: out there

WILD

jet-lagged in her red
gown she naps in the forest

cottage. three crows tap
their beaks against the metal

screen door. she sleeps onwards
but her lover hears their sounds

and knows they're enchanted
he's waiting for her to catch

up to his time zone. the wild
waits for her to come outdoors

SUMMER

the rasp-
berries are for

you. you can taste
both in your

mouth
at the same time

if you
wish

SOLITUDE

the sun surfs into
my bedroom on its high-
crest-wave of gold

barefoot I enter
the forest: green-moist
moss. I dip my

earth-darkened toes
into the lick-lapping
black-blue shimmer

the lake that I love
two blue dragonflies
bodies tight together

wing their skyway
over the water's surface.
just above the tree line

my lover's bed linen
is animal-alive in
the upward breeze:

these white and rose storm-
clouds pass me by
but pelt hail into the city:

the split-open thunder
an identical electric
storm on a far continent

delays a man's commuter
train. he runs through
the rain with no umbrella

LANGZAAM

now each
petal, stamen
pistol

we follow the bees
back to their hives
and this year for

the first time we find
a small sign: honey
we carry the jar home

eventually we'll lose
our zintuigen but until
then they lead us

on their leashes
your hand in my hair
the owl-swoosh above

our heads rain on our
tongues lavender and
the olfactory

the trees in their
upside-down
reflections

you navigate me through
Schubert's *Moments
Musicaux* as if
I was a lesser black-

backed gull
translocated west-
wards outside of
my migratory

corridor. you show
me how to use
my body to
follow the clues

so that I don't lose
my way. in the bird
scientist's bedroom
a plastic *Apis mellifera*

hangs from the ceiling
his apiologist calls
it his zombie
I've been

inhabiting
In a Landscape
by Cage and today
you unpack his *Dream*

for me as I spread
balsam honey
on ginger-almond bread
for you

LEVY FLIGHT PATTERNS

under the skylight
in his urban
office she finds

feathers
as though he's
been turning

himself into
a bird. the routes
his mind travels (while calculating

the mathematical formulas
of bird migratory patterns)
are the routes that birds

take while foraging:
over and over he retraces his thoughts
with digressions and diversions

until he discovers
new unknown ways of behaving: the Sahara
and the sea

as barriers.
when he's away a bird
falls into his office:

its fear traces
a trail
of droppings. she

covers the bird
in a bed sheet
and lifts

it back to the light
where she hopes it will find
its natural route home

Copper Thunderbird inhabits
your inner world and
spreads his wings

in your lungs. He guided your
childhood though you didn't know
this then. How could you

have known? In the city
forest a grey heron flies at
eye level right in front of your face

and you can almost reach out
and touch her wings.
In the wilderness this

would never happen. Perhaps the heron
sees Thunderbird inside
you and thinks you're a bird.

Thunderbird painted
bold colours on craft
paper and all those hues

reach you today as Michalis
sings music from the middle
ages in an Utrecht church

where the columns are
spirals of green
and rose and gold and after

he drives you along
the river where the tree-gold
and sunset-rose sweep their

stained hands into the water
and later the full moon travels a path
over the canals where behind

glass you eat watermelon ice-cream
and you tell Michalis about reading
your eleven year old self's journals

where you noted
your paper route and going door
to door: the dangerous

miners and wild lone dogs
you always (somehow)
skirted

racing along pulling the sled
you painted *Snowflake*
loaded down with the daily

news and you saved
the quarters in
a cookie tin

for the future
you would later
bite into

FALCO ELEONORAE

falco eleonorae glides
off the Greek island cliffs
large and slender, long

narrow wings. most of
the year eleonorae feeds
on butterflies, locusts

beetles, and dragonflies
but when breeding
she switches her diet

at dawn the migrating
songbirds cross the sea
song feeding the poet

ARROW STORK

May 21, 1822

we submerge our secret
loves in ponds, they bend
the reeds and sink, or we
send them to the moon
in full flight. often they
return with the spring.
years later one of
these loves returns
alive but impaled with a
central African spear
and then we know
that love doesn't hide
but flies freely away to
the south, migrating
back by choice with
the warmth even
when severely
harmed by other
more distant loves

VERTEBRAE OF HUMANS
AND ART ANIMALS

the breeze against my back
       as I cycle through narrow
              streets where tattooed

men stroll and when
       I make a wrong
              turn I'm face to

face with a sculpture
       of Mandela and the real
              Desmond Tutu stepping

down from the podium
       photographers swarm
              but I'm unable to stop

since I'm racing
       against time to a stretch
              of beach where I film

the strandbeest
       small sails as wings
              and multiple legs

the skeletal animal
       all plastic bone
              races forward

frangible
      how easily
            it topples

on my route home I watch
      an old man place a metal
            ladder against

the barbed wire fence
      he hangs a bird feeder
            up as high as he can reach

in the center a young friend
      (attacked by a mob) undergoes
            surgery

vertebrae, scapulae,
      phalanges
            osteo-sculpture

which bones
      fit where
            ossicles of

ear
   tympani
      a wave a wind lifted leaf

under a tree a woman shows
      her children how to read
            the tally marks

and tells them this is
        how many thousands of
                days Mandela

had to wait to hear
        bird song
                when his

captors knew
        exactly how
                fragile bone is

BIRDING

In my city life
I descend
the stairs in

a long
flowing dress:
there's a note

on the bottom step.
I stoop to read
the handwriting

and the neighbour
rushes out:
"It's for the man

upstairs. I hope
he'll help me.
There's a black

bird in my
pond. I'm afraid of
death."

I say, "I can help you.
Do I need
to change?"

"No," she says,
"I have a net
and a bucket."

I fish the bird out of
the pond the size of her
kitchen window.

We walk across
the street to the
meter wide ribbon

of forest.
We rest the
bird there.

HOW NOT TO HATE A PIGEON

She beckons Bruckner to surpass the pigeons
their persistence. And as always he does.
Summer sends slender arms past the blinds

and forces the windows to stay propped
wide: heat. It's too early to rise.
She tosses in the thin sheet, until the day points

a tanned arm and sends her direct to the shore
where she meets a cello player. He waves
toward the sandwich and crested terns

and shows her how to tell one from the other.
She asks him, "How do I kill a pigeon?" He says
"I thought you were a pacifist?" "Does

that have to include unmusical birds?"
"Of course," he says. Swimming, she finds
Bruckner in the sea foam and asks him

"Anton, did you hate pigeons?" "Of course
not," he says. "God forgot to add the right
colours to their timbre. That's not their fault now is it?"

Some people have
copilots. My copoet and
I clean. We

wipe the dust from the white
radiator in a comfortable
quiet way as if our source

of warmth was a sculpture
or the octave
leaps in Schubert's adagio

of the C minor sonata:
the metal slats as connected notes
with air

between. There's room
for a grand piano but
how could we carry it up

three flights
of tight stairs? One
of the other artists

asks, "Why do you need such a
large atelier if you are
writers?" For the expansive

view out onto the
trees in the sheltered
courtyard, the cathedral spire

in the distance and at street
level two empty benches under the
bare limbs, our grandiose thoughts

and ideas, our small
brief words. The fire
escape leading down

to the world below for when
our minds fall into
flame. Wild-

fires scorch entire forests
down and there are no
escape routes, only

emergency airlifts
with military pilots at the controls
where we sat strapped in two

long cargo rows
wondering if our
homes were already

torched – today I jump out
the atelier window
onto the fire escape and wipe

down the panes from
outside and
our skies clear –

FORK .

You cycle past the
French pastry shop
and ask me if

they have lemon
tarts. I say, Of
course, and we

share one with
two forks. Lemony
Snicket tweets

admiration for
your poetry and I have
a vague idea

he's a famous
author, and
an even vaguer

idea of how one
tweets. I buy more
lemon tarts as our

celebratory treat
and this time
we use one fork.

MODERN

muses are the
men who sit
in office towers
surrounded by
stacks of files
and the glow of
screens and their
agendas have
no beginnings
and no
endings and they
dream of
those free
wheeling
women out
and about
wording
on their
bicycles
and they'll meet up
for coffee
at the foot of
emergency
exit stairwells
and after the women
will race through the busy
streets with their
newly found
stanzas

MUSINGS

my mind is a tree

you are the match
and you burn me
right down to the

heart-grey ground

If he looks out his window into the linden tree,
he'll see not an angel or a ghost, but a poet mumbling
words to herself: leaves in her hair, scratches
on her arms and legs. She's a bit out of practice it seems.
Her mother always hated when she climbed
trees: her pretty hand-made dresses would get all tore up
but she had taught her mother that poets-in-training
required ready action clothes. Skirts were useless
since the boys would spend all their time
lying on the ground trying to stare up into the fabric.
She needed to kick ass, and slacks were the only
way to go. But that was years before she learned
that some boys were trained as librarians:
they were keepers of her treasures.
Like the grey-haired man surrounded
by books, wearing glasses and shuffling papers.
Was it possible that he was murmuring
to himself? She starts to eat the flowers
from the tree: their sweet honey-like flavour.

CARPENTRY

I would have to
find some suitable

trees, cut them down
it would take a

year to air dry
the wood and

then I'd have to
plane and joint

quarter saw
the planks would

point to the center
of the tree

yielding boards
that are less

prone to warp
or cup I would

slowly build this
desk for you so

that on its surface
you could taste

the almonds
from the tree

WHILE STANDING ON GOLDEN RAIN
TREE STREET

you told me about
the golden rain
tree that grew in

your childhood garden
and how this makes you
think about your girlfriend's

diabetic urine: extra
yellow and sweet. days
later she lifts her blouse

for me and shows me
the electronic gadget
pinned into her skin:

it talks to her phone
when her sugar is too
high or too low. you show

me hermaphrodite
flowers cascading their
open golden mouths on

a night of downpours
thunder and lightning
and extreme heat

On the train the cellist, poet and
composer each hold
a small pink lady

apple as if they're shot glasses and clink
them one against the other to wish
the composer a happy birthday.

He's covered in seeds, and the poet
says, laughing, that no he's not
seedy. The plants he holds

in his hand are a gift from the violinist:
yellow rattle, lupine and plantago.
As poet and composer kiss goodbye

at the end station, he says he has to
buy parsley, and the Greek word
means a plant growing

next to stone. He will cook his
birthday meal as he thinks of how
he'll add sound to an old silent

movie. At four a.m. the poet, unable to sleep
opens the balcony door and looks up
and down the silent empty street.

She sits on her red sofa and holds
a Crete pebble in her hand. It's then
that the doorbell rings twice. Who

is out there in the night?
She'll never know. By the time
she's at her front door

the bell-ringer has vanished.
She returns to her bed where
she dreams of a meadow of golden

flowers looking like tiny turtles
hatching from their eggs, and
in this field is a single apple tree.

SHELTER

we meet in a
space called cyber
pure surreality until

we walk from opposite
sides into a domed greenhouse
with palm trees and two

grand pianos: the weaving together
of Chopin, Ligeti, and Godowsky
so that the disparate gives us

a single vision: how different
our lives have been. the rooftop
rain augments the score

and drips on the mice
racing between
our feet. we become

real to each other
as we watch the musicians
receive jars of linden honey

BOULEZ CONDUCTS BLUEBEARD

He's almost two heads shorter than the soprano
as she sings about Bluebeard's seven doors.
I lived in a small fishing village where a woman
drove a VW Beetle with *Boulez* as her licence

plate. One night she drove drunk, lost
her licence and had to move into the city leaving
her dream of meeting Boulez behind. Unknowingly
she opened the seventh door for me: it was time

to abandon my third husband: he had kept
too many secrets from me. I no longer
live in Ecum Secum, but in a European city

with husband number four. Be careful what you choose
for your licence plate: Boulez is up there
right now in front of me moving his hands.

DATE WARP

Mathias rolls dates
in thyme. Bobby pops
sugared ginger into
his mouth and says, This
is like an edible
orgasm, and then he stands
up and begins to play the Steinway:
Brahms, Schönberg, and Schumann
from Z to A which is not a garbled time
warp backwards but Scherzinger's freshly
written score bringing us forward into the *now*
of things: alterations and additions
so the music is eerily familiar
and fabulously new. My lipstick
roses on the table:
petals fresh
from the street below.

into my cage, I taste
Lorca on my lips. why
had I forgotten

the stars? during
all those summers
the water stroked

my skin as I swam
in the night's mirror
note after note

the stars inked
on the score
sheets of the sky

and when I play
their songs
owls

call me from
the dark opposite
shore

MUSIC

she sees treble clefs
in the nature reserve
as she cycles past

her silver graffiti
on the trash can
water pipe cap

notes are there
too in the air
in full flight so

that her lips
begin to mimic
wing beats as a

way of waiting
for what he's
writing at night

by hand while
the light flows out
into his garden

the river tears into the banks
sweeps away small boats
large houses, cars, a horse,
a field, a clarinet, a church

organ and a swan
escapes flying overhead
and it is weeks and months
before the rains stop and

Michalis is wet, exhausted
tossed up on a far shore holding
his new score
in his hand, his head

resting on soggy tufts
of meadow and grass and
the fresh seedpods
spilling out their black peas

OP. 19   NO. VI

enl

arg   es

fragments
of
feelings

scarcely
audible
whisper

int
ima
teb

fragments
of
feelings

scarely
audible
whisper

scarcely
audible
whisper

enl

arg

54

rev
ity   exp   ress

sof   tly

fragments
of
feelings

scarcely
audible
whisper

fragments
of
feelings

viewed
under
high
res   ol

uti   on
micro
scope

rao rdi nar y

ext

55

SWEPT

her brother William melted
metal in the room
next to her kitchen
and after casting
telescope mirrors
hand polished
them nonstop for sixteen
hours as Caroline
fed him hand to
mouth she felt
her scarred face
and stunted figure
deterred male
desire yet
she welcomed Haydn
and Byron
as her guests, found
eight comets
and trailed
her thoughts in
mathematical and
musical notes
her solo
soprano concerts
her catalogue
of nebulae
she swept
the entire sky

EQUINOX

House as constellation in the sky,
and dog the space our souls inhabit
while we trespass on the earth. Does
it have to be the other way around?

Count the equal hours of light
and then darkness as the sand trickles
into the glass globe
below: REM

where all our memories
weigh the same, undivided: if we sleep
in a shared bed our brain waves
swap ideas across the short

expanse between our feather pillows,
individual dreams that create immeasurable
new patterns. Outside splashes
of flaming red flowers

fringe the rice paddies marking
our path into autumn: tomorrow
we visit our ancestors' graves.
Red Equinox Flower: Higanbana:

plant, you have no sense
of restraint when it comes to sex,
throwing chromosomes
around with total abandon.

But unlike you, sterile red Lycoris radiata
our ancestors merged egg/sperm
and passed on their hopes
and nightmares

to each of us. The bedroom
doors stand open
onto all the constellations
and in pre-sleep: sleep: we multiply

each other's heavens.

LUZ

they watch seven pallid
swifts floating in
formation and at night

from within
the darkness
she opens the small

square window onto
the moonlight and he says
she's a beautiful

nude black and white
photo and she says
the best things

are never words
except when written
on the body

as he begins
to play *A Dog's Life*
along her spine

FRED'S DOG

The dog bites
my left boot
in the Belgium
café. It's not
Fred's dog
because he doesn't
own a dog, but
he just wrote a new
piano concerto
called *A Dog's Life*
and the pianist
says, "I'm being led
along by
the leash."
Fred says,
"The dog gets
excited by this and
that odour and goes
running from tree
to tree moving
rapidly from one
to the next."
Fred's wearing
a hand-knit sweater
with a backpacker
on the front. The pianist
says he's been cross-
country skiing
in Germany, and

Japanese tourists
took his photo.
A tourist from
the next table
says to us, "We heard
you talking.
We're from Texas."
Fred says, "No you're
not." The woman
says, "You're right.
We've only lived there
for three years.
We're from Ohio."
The man says,
"Have a good
trip." None of us are
returning to
the Americas. We look
at each other
talking with our
eyes. Later
in bed my
brain is
still walking
Fred's dog, but
I don't tell
my lover this.

COMING

my lover laughs
at me since all
the dogs even when

sighting me from a long
distance race straight
toward me to drool

and lick and sniff and
today in the city
forest I see two large white

dogs and they see me
but they race skittishly
sideways back and forth

among the trees and jewel
weed and I look about
for the owner

to say your dogs
are gorgeous and
a young

blond man steps out
from behind
a tree and I know now

what his dogs knew, she's coming
your way, and when I turn
to gaze back

the larger of the dogs is
pissing in the same way against
the exact same spot

WINTER

Snow

falls

where

in a country

Feldman's [ ]

[is not heard]

notes

does not [ ]

[ ]play

People slide

play

in a

canal

snow

where

[are not]

through the slush:

64

sloosh:

stillness: < the sound <oh Feldman: > the sound of >

the car slithers:

a boy falls

on the ice

his mobile

snow

People build snow< >: the

and still

ings

one on top

other spaced

out in the park field

snow[o]men

are Feldman's

[impro....] stacked

NOCTURNES

during
winter months
of insomnia

Frederic inks
three nocturnes
hoping sleep will

reach him like a gift
dropped through
the mail slot

like a feather
fallen from a
blue wing, like the

memory of the sunset
slipping through
the late evening blinds

like the midnight
train where the two single
men, the couple,

the family with children
all have their
eyes shut, a few soft

snores and Frederic
with his head
against the window

also falls away
from the world
as he hurtles

toward a destination
whose address he
often fails to find

BLIZZARD

her lover coughed for
seven days and nights

and then left on
a necessary journey.

the migrant
workers next door

pack their bandsaw
into their truck and drive

off. she swigs down
the stillness they

all left behind. later
at her piano she feels

Rzewski's newly
written *Winter Nights*.

who can hear
her? even those

closest to her
are unable to travel

her thoughts.
she forgets to fasten

windows and snow-
flakes slip in

LULLABY

Webern's *Kinderstück*
was played in public
for the first time

by a nine year old girl.
at the top of the score
pianists are guided

not by *Sehr Langsam*
or *Etwas Rasch* but *Lieblich.*
Webern, wishing

to avoid
disturbing
his grandchildren

stepped out
into the street to smoke
his cigar:

an edgy soldier
shot him. trained
and ready, he didn't hear

in the necessary
moment the essential
song. a lost lullaby

slips between
my lips: let my
eye in the night

be the vision of a wick
and may you
be blind

enough to light it
and when we flare
let all soldiers

and all world
hatreds be ever
absent:

let the altering
be in the rhythm
of the carotid

pulse: *Sehr Rasch.*
asleep, I watch you
step before

my house
and listen
to the notes

fall deep
into the melting snow
the ice-cold

that you
whistled
away

you meet me at the top
of the west stairs where
I'm a rainbow raincoat in
the rushing crowd. we're
surrounded by water
but remain on land with
our thoughts floating
swirling all around
us. a white paper boat is
a lantern in the night and
shines on the sea entering
your city where light
in all its colours funnels
into streams. we cross
the street where a composer
whose name is heart
and a violinist who
is a Faust bring forth
music in the cold drafty
aisles where I warm you
with my red scarf. hidden
in the after crowd is
a homeless man simply
seeking heat on the
indoor bench. we walk
the gang plank an
architect placed there
for us, and we feel the
ongoing open wind

and the rustle and swirl
of its northerly notes
touches our unclasped
hands. these nights are
the unlit lantern wicks of
our lives and we store
them in polished glass
jars open to the sky

NOVEMBER

white feather curls
upward on the black
water a calm so
absolute the world
duplicates itself
rocks no longer
triangles but rhomboids
more alluring
than their usual
wave-splashed
selves always
we serve as
mirrors for
each other
faces memories
how this late
autumn surpasses
summer precisely
because of the lake's bold
edge, this frost-engraved
ice that I navigate
through in my
canoe to the sound
of a hundred champagne
glasses smashed
against the hearth
and melting into
the home warmth
where you'll hold
my blue feet in your
glowing hands

CLASP THE SHIMMER

as the plunging light rips
        the blue-black waves

on the flat rock marked *here*
        your indigo dress, crumpled
                memory

soon all the trees
        will be stolen for doors
                the fallen pieces of sky

we call windows
        reveal only
                a patch of all

possible views
        courage leads swimmers
                home – not away, breast

stroke by breast stroke –

THIS

you swim alone
at sunset in the North Sea
leaving nothing on
shore but a skirt
and a sweater and you own
nothing but the memorized
love letter in your mind
and the song residing
in your heart though of course this
is not a ship on the water
sailing with your own but
a knowing and a
known
for you own
not your life nor
the shoes at your door

it was in a dream
but Socrates did
serve you breakfast
of quince, yogurt and honey
and on your bedroom
wall hung a Greek sonnet
framed in gold. in the early
morning the elderly
priest struck bells
as the hammer on metal
of his work day: you swam
out as far as
you could reach
and it was far enough

LATE SUMMER

tiny fish so blue
and fresh it's the slice
of sky gasping in the sand
next to the orange fallen
from a ship
further inland
the rosehips
red-ripe are plump on their own
Vitamin C
and seeds
a fast-black dog
(but not fast enough)
races after
a rabbit
on the leaf-gold edge
of the cycling trail
and the sunset tug
of longing
breathes
gilled inside
of her

TRANSLUCENT

Hyalinobatrachium pellucidum

in the remote
mountains of Ecuador
species after species are
(re)discovered. the glass

frog through its translucent skin
shows us its internal
organs. we keep thoughts
tucked not beneath layers

of skin or clothing but
beneath the (un)spoken
we're unable to quantify
love when it finds us

so unexpectedly
together after
thirty-three years
our essential

feelings held
in the hand
like an orange
that has fallen

The tall gorgeous man says
softly, "Do you want
one?" I've been
standing still for a long time
staring up into the
tree. He opens
his palm to show me
the orange he's
peeling. He thinks
I'm longing
for the same, but
am too short to reach
high. He's right of
course. Why do I live
exiled from the shine
of oranges? Behind
us is the flower
bed memorial
for all of us who
have been harmed throughout
history: red
flowers and one
pink blossom spread
out in an arrow
reaching forward. I nod
yes to
the man and he plucks
an orange and places
it in my palm and

we smile at each
other and walk away in
different directions
eating from
the same tree.

AT THE CAFÉ

you and I walk down the long
hospital corridor with Cavafy
in my packsack and you sit

still for over an hour listening
intensely as the doctor asks
me questions, as he touches

my abdomen, breast, legs
and when we leave
I have four lab

bottles for my body
fluids in my packsack
and they clatter and chatter

with Cavafy in the autumn
sun as we walk through
the city to my favorite café

where we sit on the bridge
at the square table with
the loose board and you

read Cavafy and my hand
doesn't touch your brow, lips
and eyes but the light does

INTIMATE

what upsets her most
of all is having to wake
the doctor's teenage son
each morning by touching
his shoulder: his anger thrown
at her. she's unable to decipher
the foreign words, the news
about the lawyer who wanted
to grant her
freedoms, who
just died after a long
illness. she has no health
insurance, no identity
papers. she knows the
nailheads in the floorboards,
the soft dust at the foot
of table legs, the daughter's
long strands of hair
drifting across the hand polished
hardwood, the undersides of
bed frames

I walk through
the garden of
the body. Did

Erasmus know
about Euphrasia?
I am made of glass

or, if possible,
something even
more fragile

than glass.
In the garden
within the

garden, I stand
inside the fever
house: roofless

and built from
eyeglass lenses.
Everything is

blurred until
I float a feather
and Latin words

on water mirrors
for you: *Difficilia
Quae Pulchra.*

Flower-beds
shaped like leaves:
habitat of muses

the garden is our library
open to the sky:
Sidera Addere Caelo:

sleep: you awaken
to find poppies
on your pillowcase.

CORPUSCLES

when a bird
flies in the
darkening

sky the air
it moves with
its wing-beats

enters my lungs
and the fresh
oxygen

channels through
my heart so that
each thought

is a boat
moving in
my body the red

blood cells
with their white
sails

he tells her the blood
work her doctor needs
to do because he knows

about the body along
with his busyness with ancient
musical manuscripts

curating a love
story, handwriting
and long ago gifts

stored safe in vitrines
while her cells
are being viewed

under microscopic
slides she visits him
with her newly

written score
so that he can hear
the real but why

is the past less real
than the present
when even ghosts

breathe in a tangible
way so that he feels
the air on the back

of his neck move
as if he's just
been kissed there

BREATHING

in the Balinese
jungle the tigers are real
but only as breathing

ghosts: in their hard-bodied
energy they once prowled
beneath the swing

of the vines. the extinct
tigers admired
snakes most of

all and they've all
survived: they glide
entwine and hang

in curved loops
their beauty and their
wisdom green or brown

or blue. when
fortune is real
the snakes reveal

themselves as bangles. turn
their heads toward
your inner wrist and feel

the shape of luck
the hidden rapid
pulse

blue-green veins
and arteries *tyger
tyger, burning bright*

INSOMNIA

In Indonesia she tosses
turns as nightmares swoop
into her sleep. By day

she walks in the monsoon
jungle. Her guide is
seventy-three but

moves as if
he's forty.
He points to

a red-brick ruin
and smiles joy
over the cloud

that found
Hiroshima. A fallen
tree is their bridge

across a river.
He gestures for her
to sit on a looped

vine and pushes
her as she swings.
He shows her plants: red

dye hidden in green
leaves: flavours
for soup: edible

scents for her body.
He calls like a bird
and the birds call

back. He says next
time she can walk
the entire day with

him, next time
he'll set up a tent
for her under trees.

He says, Good sleep.
That night in her four
poster bed hung

with mosquito
netting she hears
the murmurings

of the jungle: trees
strangling other
trees in order to live, or

trees living
symbiotically.
She sleeps in soothing

green depths even if
they're depths
she'll never reach.

We read the signs
and walk through long
corridors, down flights
of stairs but the playwright's
talk is over. The organizer
apologizes about the false
times and suddenly
gestures *follow me*
and we retrace
our steps as though
we were back
on stage caught in
a perpetual repeat
of Phoenician women
witnessing murder in the next
room, the next village,
the next country:
actors in real-time played
in reverse: how long
did they train
for all that walking
backwards up
the stairs, some in
leg casts, some in slings.
The organizer loses us
in the crowd
finds us again
and brings us
to the actor's private

dining room where
we're given
gratis drinks and see
that the leg cast isn't a prop
but is merely real. Our earlier
dinner conversation about
a long letter my mother wrote
me: the rapes in
her war-childhood
village, and how she
was perhaps kept safe
as a bunch of little kids
and a younger
mother looking
like a skeleton
with all white
hair – On fast
forward I hold your
wine glass, the stem
warm as if your hand
was still there.
On stage the glass
museum cases
were carried
forwards and
backwards and forwards again
displaying knife,
stone, knife –

WITNESS

Clara, age twelve you wrote
music full of romance and immense
forward strides: your future

husband courted you by showing
you how he could improve your scores.
He visualized you playing a concert ·

but wrote that you looked more lovely
in the kitchen. You didn't visit
him when he was in hospital, but stayed

home and began
composing again, a musical love
as your full gift to him:

marriage encoded in song.
Clara, you encouraged
pianist Anna Rosbaud

and predicted a great
future for her. Anna gave
birth to four children

out of wedlock
preferring the key
that opened doors

to new choices:
never a husband.
Anna gave two

children away, but kept
the middle boys:
Hans, a famous conductor,

and Paul, spy and
friend of high
level Nazis. He secretly

sent science facts year
after year to Britain.
Paul, friend of

Lise Meitner (denied
the Nobel Prize)
who forwarded his messages

to his Jewish wife.
Paul encoded in a letter
to his brother, *I am working*

positively in other ways.
For a long time now
I have been turning

toward those
to whom the first lines
of the serious song refer.

Brahms had written *Four
Serious Songs* for
the dying

Clara Schumann:
*oppressed they
had no comfort*:

Paul gained entry
into the camps
and witnessed –

LOVE LETTERS

in her beehives
she hides
her husband's
prison letters

while an ant
drags a white
rose petal over
the rubble

SKIN

a man's frosted exhalation
in the pitch interior

of a car's trunk
is white against black

like chalk on the board
easily erased, but

not easily forgotten
the sound of tires on snow

heard from inside
the trunk of a cop car

After leaving Hungary,
Ménes travels through
Romania, Bulgaria,
Greece, Turkey, Syria,
Jordan, and Israel
and ends up in prison
in Egypt charged with
espionage. Photos
of him behind bars
circulate the global
news: half in shadow
beak lowered, toes
spread on concrete.
He's found innocent
and set free, but is
soon discovered
dead on an island
near Aswan.
Suspicious of
his satellite tag
Egyptian police
called him Swan
but his real surname
was Stork.

WINTER COAT

during a thunder and
lightning storm a family

crosses the border
the six year old

girl is soaking
wet and freezing

a soldier gives her
dry fresh clothing

and the father
takes the winter

jacket and defecates
on it saying his daughter

must never have better
clothing than his own

after the bombs
a woman tells me
how she saw a man
in a bulky jacket and

she stood up to move
to another compartment
but the train is full of
men from warm countries

in big winter coats
and a man with new
gold-rim eyeglasses
says when he's alone

at night on the street
he's even more afraid
when he sees a young
man walking towards

him and I say, you mean
a man who doesn't look
like you? and he says
yes, he could be

dissatisfied and angry
and a young man
sits down in front of
me and the woman next

to him gets up and
moves to the front
of the bus and
the young man turns

to me and says, this
moving away from us
when it's us who
have lived and fled

what they fear
and in the city forest
a young man
in a bulky coat stands

for a long time
in a pool of spring light
looking at the softness
of the flowers

WINGS

two strangers in the city forest
stand watching grey herons
three in a row in the cool shade

slowly the birds are forgotten
as one man swears refugees are lowering
his pension and the other says

softly he's a human rights lawyer:
one man's right wing and the other
left: two metal wings land

in a field of wildflowers
in eastern Ukraine and coal miners search
for fragments of

what was briefly
known as flight:
our human

remains. rebels
rush to hide
the evidence. why

do we shoot the flight
of our dreams from the sky?
a Bali guidebook rests

beneath a sunflower.
no bird flies
with only one wing

THREADS

A young refugee boy
Zahi's new friend

comes over to brush
his hands through

Zahi's thick wavy
hair. Zahi says, "It was

longer before" and shows
us a photo on his

mobile phone where he sits
in a lush green landscape.

Zahi fled from Lebanon
to Egypt and then a dangerous

smuggler-boat journey
to Italy and by car to

the Netherlands.
The boy threads

a pink and a green
straw horizontally

through Zahi's hair
with the curved ends

jutting out on each side
of Zahi's head

like pastel horns
and the boy's joyous

laughter fills our
dining room.

FOOD

I enter the refugee center and
am told to sit and wait
and I watch boxes and
boxes of fresh
food arrive and in front
of the security
gates a tall woman
says in Dutch that the food
is not allowed
and a woman in a
headscarf says in English
it's a gift and the tall
woman says she's not from
that organization
and men keep
bringing more and
more and the boxes
form stacks between
me and the gate and a man
speaks softly in Arabic
and a blond woman in
a red Santa hat joins the
crowd and young men
who have fled their
homes walk in and out
and I'm waiting to
guide seventy refugees
who wish to visit
the library but I'm now told
they've left through
the other door

Μπαλοθιά

Gunshot fired
into the air
at the feast is
my first Greek
word, not
because I was
there but you
were here
and you felt
it was the first
word I should
know. Did you
have a gun,
I ask. Of course,
you say. Why? I say.
I needed one, you say. There
are many
reasons to need
a gun. Why?
I say. I was in
the army, you say.
I had a gun when
I was twelve, I say.
It was for
food. Your great-aunt
hands out sandwiches
each day on
the island where
you served in

the army
and where refugees now come
in small fragile boats
holding maps of
their hopes in their
heads, and
they send mobile
messages,
We are
here. Where
are you?

DANCE

light out of
the sand

day after
the storm
she finds

an electric
bulb on
the shore

in her packsack
no room for
lamps, shells

or love letters
the longing
is the gesture

she brushes
the beach from
her feet

THE SHORE

where the ragged surf
touches the sand,
where birdsong

choreographs the
movement of
the air, and where

stillness is never less
than the intake
of each breath; inland

tiny purple flowers
glow-out from the green
and the stalk with

its delicate globe
of dandelion seed
when touched by the

wind (or by me)
will release
flown-messages that

will blow into your
open window
in your eastern land

MIRRORS

when the sun radiates at a late afternoon
angle, the bank building acts like a mirror

reflecting extra light into the lawyer's
office. does he see the bird

perched on the branch outside his
window? he's studying a story

for the truths or fictions that will
give a refugee a new

life. on a branch in a nearby
park a white scarf is caught

in the sunrays: a pattern of red birds on
red wires. where is the woman

who has lost this? the young refugee
watched his mother being

murdered. the man who
shot her pulled the scarf

from her head. as a child
he often watched his mother

standing in front of the
mirror combing her hair

and lost along
the shore
the gentle slope
of the hill upwards
and we are found
again only when we
recognize the war
memorial where
resistance fighters
were shot and buried
in the sand of the dunes
you were imprisoned
in your youth for being
at the wrong place at the
wrong time, for trying
to make a better world
darkness falls upon
us and there is no
better world, only
the calls of the
nameless birds
in these brief
moments when
the birds still
exist for us: the bell
in the dunes tolls
once a year to
remind us of what
we still have
to lose

OUTSIDE

It began slowly
with smiles on official
photographs becoming

forbidden. None of
us paid any
attention. What

did it matter if
we looked like our
grimmer selves?

Until suddenly we
were confronted with
prison sentences for

all public smiling, and
once you were in
jail you rarely

returned to
the outside
world. A man works

in the windowless
cold basement of the train
station repairing

our bikes.
The cameras are
pointed the other way

so I always smile at
him. Over the years
he observes

my small losses.
I arrive to discover
my purse was

stolen en route. I rush
back having forgotten
my backpack, but

he has kept it safe.
I ask him about his
bandaged wrist and

he says he fell
off his bike. We share
only a few words of

our common
foreign language, but
we understand each

others' faces.
We look into
each others' eyes.

One night late when
I return alone
he says, "Where's

your boyfriend?
I haven't seen him."
I say, "He's ill."

I've been instructed
to say this.
The man says, "Tell

him the bike repair
man sends
his greetings."

I place my hand
over my heart and
thank him. My

boyfriend smiled at me
in the public square
and now he's gone.

SONG

Grandmother tells
me how birds
used to fly in
the sky, she
shapes her
hands into wings
and sings a song
I know she's
making up stories
but I love
her and hug
her. the sky
is empty and grey
and we're not
allowed outdoors
but I have
the glow of
my screen
and my friends
are all there
I've never
met them but
who would
want to and
anyway I'm
old enough
to know they're
not real

WINDBLOWN

You are trying to sing
                              a song
that has been lost or
                    has never
                              been written

                                   you hum slowly
                         trying to find
                  the tune

my breath, her anchor
   tugs with the algae and tears –
do you hear it?

            Celan could
                         help you
                              with the words

through thought-
founts
the crane comes
swimming, taut – you open
to him

            Hart
                  Crane

with his
silken skilled
transmemberment
of song

you urgently
            need to find
                        the song
            that will sing you

out of the water:
            the river you are swimming
  in *now*

                                    your arms are not strong
enough, and you've lost the *O* in song
                        the *O* that is both the life ring
                        and the whistle

attached to the life
                    ring

                        what you have instead is
an *E* which you foolishly use
                        to comb your hair

all your life long you've never carried
                                    a comb
                        in your purse
you always arrived

                windblown
so why
                are you combing your hair now

when it has turned
                                white, now when you
are being carried

downstream by the current?
                                        swim
and use the *E*
                like a version of *W* or *M*

                                                as if these
                                                        letters
                                        are the open

arms
        of a man and a woman sitting
                                        together
on a bench on the shore
                                starry
                        crane
                        seed

OUTLINED BY LAMPS

She's late: the sun has already
set, but the air is gentle with heat
and the sky is tender with many

variants of light: ships on the
horizon are moored like distant
small villages outlined by lamps

sending messages of forgotten
Morse code. Flocks
of plovers are silhouetted by

the backdrop of orange-rose
clouds that darken moment
by moment. She had not

planned on swimming
but she slips out of
blouse, skirt and enters

the softness of the sea.
The city in the southern distance
thrums, glitters its faux necklace.

She emerges from the water
wearing seaweed and sand
as darkness cloaks her.

A few strangers step
out from the shadows, but
they too remain silent; everyone

is blind and they walk
forward by feel to the upward
slope of sand that will lead

them to their bicycles.
As small lights they move slowly
or at speed away from the dunes.

Rabbits and toads hop across
the trail; enchanted, they're turned
into alternative versions of their lives.

ACKNOWLEDGMENTS AND NOTES

Some of these poems have been performed as poetry in concert by the New European Ensemble in the Netherlands. Earlier versions of some of these poems appeared in *The Antigonish Review, Geist Magazine* (online), *Bordercrossing* (Berlin), and *Magna* (UK). "Modern" was published in *Magic Oxygen Literary Prize* 2015 (UK). "Vision" was shortlisted for the *Arc* Poem of the Year contest 2015. "On View" and "It's Not What One Expects" were shortlisted for the Bridport Poetry Prize (UK) 2015. "Intimate" was shortlisted for the Bridport Poetry Prize (UK) 2016.

"Paradise Evacuated": Paradise is a settlement in the Northwest Territories, Canada

"In a Landscape": John Cage, American composer (1912–1992)

"Boulez Conducts Bluebeard": Pierre Boulez, French composer (1925–2016)

"Date Warp": Martin Scherzinger, South African composer (1966–)

"Op. 19   No. VI": Arnold Schönberg, Austrian composer (1874–1951)

"Swept": Caroline Herschel, German Astronomer (1750–1848)

"Luz" and "Fred's Dog": *A Dog's Life* (2014) is a piano concerto written by American composer Frederic Rzewski (1938–)

"Winter": Morton Feldman, American composer (1926–1987)

"Nocturnes" and "Blizzard": *Winter Nights* (2014) are three solo piano nocturnes written by Frederic Rzewski

"Lullaby": Anton Webern, Austrian composer (1883–1945)

"This": set to music by Greek composer Michalis Paraskakis (1980–) in 2015

"November": set to music by Canadian composer Carmen Braden (1985–) in 2015

"Vision": *I am made of glass or, if possible, something even more fragile than glass.* Erasmus, Epistola 1484; *Difficilia Quae Pulchra*: good things are difficult; *Sidera Addere Caelo*: add stars to the sky.

"Witness": Clara Schumann, German composer (1819–1896)

"The Shore": set to music by Dutch composer Nico Huijbregts (1961–) in 2016

"Windblown": The italicized lines "my breath, her anchor ..." are from my translation of Paul Celan's poem "Vor Mitternacht." The lines "through thought- /founts ..." and "starry/crane/seed" are from my translation of Celan's poem "Wenn du im Bett." The lines "silken skilled ..." are from Hart Crane's poem "Voyage."

https://eleonoreschonmaier.com